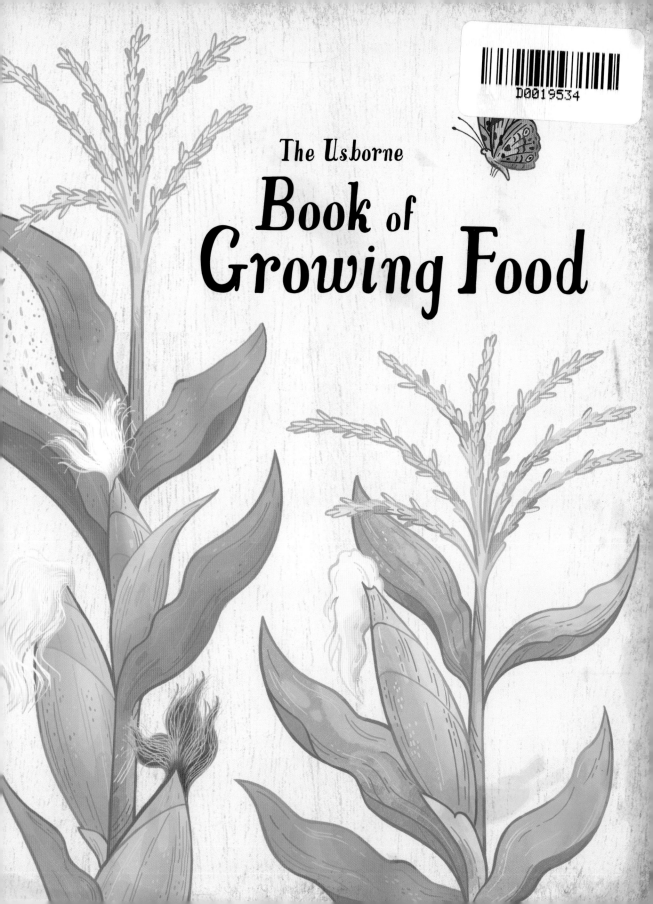

The Usborne

Book of Growing Food

The Usborne
Book of
Growing Food

Written by Abigail Wheatley

Illustrated by Anni Betts and John Russell

Designed by Hannah Ahmed, Helen Edmonds
and Vickie Robinson

Gardening expert: Hayley Young

CONTENTS

Usborne Quicklinks

For links to websites where you can find more tips
and activities for growing your own food, and watch
video clips to see how plants grow, go to the Usborne
Quicklinks website at www.usborne.com/quicklinks
and enter the keywords 'growing food'.

Please follow the internet safety guidelines
at the Usborne Quicklinks website.

BEFORE YOU START

Everything in this book is grown in containers, so you don't need a garden. A small space outside, such as a sunny windowsill or balcony, is fine for many of the projects. Others can be grown inside.

Before you start growing, read the tips and techniques section at the end of this book. Then, read through the project to make sure you have everything you need.

How to use this book:

When and where to start growing

Everything you need

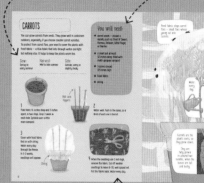

Step-by-step instructions

How to harvest – pick, pull up or gather what you've grown when it's ready to eat.

Check with your local gardening center or cooperative extension office for more advice on plant varieties and soil needs for your area.

Don't use sprays or chemicals on your plants, except where a projects tells you to.

Soil Safety

Getting dirt or compost in your eyes, or in cuts or scratches can make you sick. Cover any cuts or scratches with an adhesive bandage before you start. If they're on your hands, wear gardening gloves.

If you cut or scrape yourself while gardening, wash the cut right away and cover with a bandage.

Don't ever touch the droppings of animals such as dogs and cats.

For more gardening safety tips, go to www.usborne.com/quicklinks

Eating what you grow

Find recipe ideas for eating and cooking the things you grow on the Usborne Quicklinks website: www.usborne.com/quicklinks

All the things you need to buy are easy to find in garden centers or other stores.

If you see a word you don't know, check it in the glossary on pages 62-63.

EQUIPMENT

Before you start a growing project, read through the instructions to make sure you have gathered together all the plants, tools and equipment you will need.

Wear gardening gloves when dealing with tough or scratchy stems.

They also protect you from plants that might irritate your skin, such as strawberries or squash.

Watering cans can be heavy, so use a small one or half-fill a big one.

Use the size and shape of container that each project recommends.

Some things grow inside glass jars.

For watering seeds and seedlings, attach a 'rose' to make the water pour more gently.

Unless a project says otherwise, use containers with drainage holes. These stop plants from getting waterlogged.

Use string to tie around canes.

A pencil is handy for poking holes in grow bags and writing on labels.

When using plant pots indoors, put a drip tray underneath.

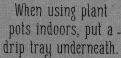

A fork can be handy for harvesting.

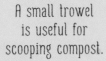
A small trowel is useful for scooping compost.

A pair of pruning shears might be helpful for cutting thicker stems.

Scissors are useful for cutting things such as string, netting or thin plant stems.

Top bamboo canes with toppers – you can buy them or use upside-down yogurt containers or snail shells. This stops people from getting hurt if they walk into them.

Some projects ask for liquid plant food. Follow the mixing instructions on the packaging.

You could make your own plant food – see page 61.

Bamboo canes support plant stems and give vines something to grow up.

Many projects ask for multi-purpose compost. Don't use ordinary garden soil, as it might not be the right type to help your plants grow.

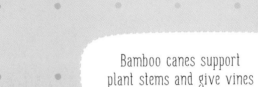

You can make your own compost – see page 60.

Plant labels are useful to remind you what you've planted.

THINGS TO GROW

On the following pages, you'll find step-by-step instructions on how to grow all kinds of different food, from sprouting beans and edible flowers, to squash shaped like flying saucers.

CARROTS

You can grow carrots from seeds. They grow well in containers outdoors, especially if you choose smaller carrot varieties. To protect from carrot flies, you need to cover the plants with frost fabric — a thin fabric that lets through water and light but nothing else. It helps to keep the plants warm too.

Sow:
Spring to early summer

Harvest:
Mid to late summer

Site:
Outside, sunny or slightly shady

You will need:

★ carrot seeds — choose a variety such as Short N' Sweet, Parmex, Oxheart, Little Finger, or Nantes

★ a plant pot at least 12 inches deep, filled with multi-purpose compost

★ 3 canes around 12 inches high

★ frost fabric

★ string

1

Poke holes ½ inches deep and 3 inches apart, in two rings. Drop 3 seeds in each hole. Sprinkle over a little more compost on top.

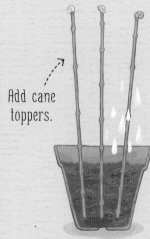

Add cane toppers.

2

Water well. Push in the canes, so a third of each one is buried.

3

Cover with frost fabric tied on with string. Water every day through the fabric. In 1-2 weeks, seedlings will appear.

String

4 When the seedlings are 1 inch high, remove the fabric. Cut off weaker seedlings to leave 8-10, well spaced out. Put the fabric back. Water every day.

Frost fabric stops carrot flies – small flies whose young eat into carrots.

If you need to remove the fabric, do it in the evening. Carrot flies aren't around then.

Water every day.

Carrots are the plant's roots, so they grow down.

They are fully grown in around two months, when the leaves are tall and bushy.

Harvesting

Remove the fabric. Grasp a bunch of leaves, pull, and the carrot will come out with the leaves.

Then, cover the pot with fabric again.

SHALLOTS

Shallots are a type of small onion. When you plant one in a container outside, a bunch of new shallots will grow from it. Buy shallots intended for planting, not for eating, known as sets.

Plant:
Late winter to early spring

Harvest:
Summer

Site:
Outside, sunny

1 Plant the sets, spacing them evenly. Push them in so just the tips show. Water well.

Plant this way up.

2 Push in the canes along the sides of the container, then tie string between the canes, like this. This will stop birds from getting to the shallots and eating them.

Add cane toppers.

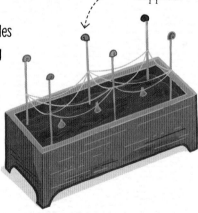

3 Check twice a week and water if dry. After 4-6 weeks, leaves will appear. Keep watering twice a week.

★ 3 shallot sets — choose a variety such as Ambition, French Red, Conservor, Dutch Red

★ a long container such as a windowbox around 20 inches long, 4 inches wide and 6 inches deep, filled with multi-purpose compost

★ 6 short garden canes or sticks with cane toppers

★ string

Potential problems

Pale green or yellow patches on the leaves might be onion downy mildew. To help avoid it, don't splash water on the leaves and leave plenty of space around the container.

Leaving plenty of space is also a good way to avoid a disease called rust. It makes brown speckles on the leaves.

BUSH BEANS

Bush beans are compact and will grow well in a container. You can grow them outdoors from seeds.

Sow:
Late spring to early summer

Harvest:
Late summer

Site:
Outside, sunny but not windy

You will need:

★ bush bean seeds — choose varieties such as Blue Lake, Bush Kentucky Wonder, Romano Purpiat, Royalty Purple or Purple Teepee

★ a plant pot at least 12 inches wide and deep, filled with multi-purpose compost

★ a pencil

★ liquid tomato food

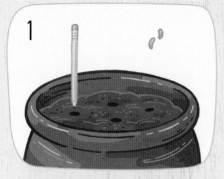

1

Use a pencil to poke 4 holes in the compost, around 1½ inches deep. Drop 2 seeds in each hole. Sprinkle a little more compost over the top. Water well.

Potential pests

Keep slugs and snails off your beans — see page 58 for tips. Wipe off aphids (see page 59), or grow chives nearby — see pages 50–51.

2
Check the compost every other day and water if it's dry. In 1-2 weeks, seedlings will appear.

3 Pull out the smaller, weaker seedlings of each pair, to leave 4 seedlings. Keep on watering every other day if necessary.

Flowers appear, then fade. Then beans grow in their place.

Harvesting

When the beans are around 5 inches long, snip them off carefully.

If it's cold, wrap the plant loosely in frost fabric.

Water every other day if dry. Once flowers appear, add liquid tomato food to the water once a week (follow the instructions on the packaging).

Most varieties are green, but some are purple or yellow. The seed packet will tell you.

SPROUTING BEANS

When a bean or other seed first starts to grow, a tiny, pale shoot sprouts out of it after just a few days. These are good to eat when you grow them in the way shown here.

Start:
Anytime

Harvest:
1–4 days after starting

Site:
Inside, light and airy but not in direct sun

You will need:

★ beans or seeds from a supermarket or health food store — choose varieties such as chick peas, mung beans, pumpkin seeds, sunflower seeds or alfalfa seeds (look for packets sold for sprouting)

★ a clean glass jar

★ a pair of old, clean panty hose that you can cut up

★ a rubber band that fits snugly around the mouth of your jar

★ ¼ teaspoon of salt

★ a tray

1 Fill the jar ⅓ full of beans or seeds. Stretch part of the panty hose over the top. Put the rubber band around the jar mouth. Cut off the excess fabric.

2 Pour in enough water to fill the jar. Add the salt and stir until it dissolves. Pour into the jar through the panty hose. Leave for 8 hours.

Potential problems

Always rinse sprouting beans once a day and wash them well before eating. If there's any sign of mold, don't eat the beans and throw them away.

3 Turn the jar over in the sink, to drain the water off. Fill with fresh water, gently swirl it around, then pour it out again. Put the jar on a tray in a light place, propped at an angle so more water can drain off.

Every morning and night, fill the jar with water. Swirl it around, then tip it to drain off all the water.

Try sprouting several different types of beans or seeds at the same time.

Mixed seeds

Pumpkin seeds

Alfalfa

Shoots sprout in 1-4 days, depending on the type of bean or seed.

Chick peas

Harvesting

Eat the beans no later than two days after they sprout.

When they're ready to eat, wash them well and put in a clean jar in the refrigerator.

PEAS IN A POT

Peas are actually seeds, so when you plant them outdoors they grow into plants and produce *more* peas. Buy peas that are specifically for growing. Peas for eating are unlikely to grow, especially if they've been frozen. They are vines, so they need pea netting (a plastic mesh) to climb up as they grow.

Sow:
Early spring

Harvest:
Early summer

Site:
Outside, sunny

1 Wrap the rubber band around the canes. Spread out the cane ends. Push them down into the planter. Drape the netting around the canes. Tie it on with string.

Add cane toppers.

2 Water the compost. Plant peas around the edge, 4 inches apart and 1 inch deep. Push the compost over the holes to cover them.

3 Water well. Check every few days and water if dry. After 2 weeks, seedlings will appear.

You will need:

★ peas for planting — choose a compact bush variety such as Peas in a Pot, Sugar Ann, or Tom Thumb

★ a planter at least 12 inches wide and tall, filled with multi-purpose compost

★ 3 canes around 31 inches high with cane toppers

★ rubber band

★ pea netting

★ string

★ liquid tomato food

Potential problems

White, powdery patches on leaves may be powdery mildew — a fungus. Keep your peas well-watered to avoid it.

Aphids will sometimes eat pea vines, but you can get rid of them with insecticidal soap.

Birds sometimes steal pods and eat pea shoots. If this is a problem, use bird netting (see page 59).

Flowers will appear, then fade. Pea pods will grow in their place.

The growing plants climb up the netting.

After the flowers fade, water every other day (every day if it's hot). Every 10-14 days add liquid tomato food to the water (follow the instructions on the packaging).

Harvesting

The peas are ready when the pods are plump and firm. Pick each pod by pulling it gently.

HERBS FROM CUTTINGS

With some types of herbs, you can make a new plant by taking a piece from an existing plant, known as a cutting. Start it inside. Later, you can move it outdoors if you like. The method is the same for both mint and rosemary.

Plant:
Spring to
early summer

Harvest:
Summer to fall

Site:
Sunny, inside
or outside

You will need:

★ access to an existing rosemary plant or mint plant

★ a plant pot around 2½ inches wide filled with multi-purpose compost, plus a drip tray

★ a pencil

★ a jar

★ a plant pot at least 3½ inches wide filled with multi-purpose compost, plus a drip tray

1 Pull off a piece around 2½ inches long from the main stem of a mint or rosemary plant. Try to leave a little bit of the main stem on the piece. Pull off the leaves at the bottom.

2 Half-fill the jar with water and put in the cutting. Leave it on a sunny windowsill and wait for the cutting to grow roots.

3 When the roots are long and thick, use the pencil to poke a hole in the compost. Put the cutting in the hole and push compost around it.

4 Check every few days and water if dry. When roots show under the pot, repot the plant into the larger pot (see how on page 56).

To make your plant bushy, cut the tips off long stems. More stems will grow.

Outside, rosemary likes a very sunny spot. Mint doesn't mind shade for some of the day.

Keep on watering every few days, if dry.

Wait until your plant has grown big and strong before harvesting.

Harvesting

Cut off the top 2 inches of a few stems.

EDIBLE FLOWERS

Some flowers have petals you can eat. They look pretty added to salads, or floating on top of drinks such as lemonade. Try growing edible flowers in a planter outdoors.

Sow:
Spring

Harvest:
Summer to
early fall

Site:
Outside, sunny

You will need:

★ nasturtium seeds (*Tropaeolum majus* or *Tropaeolum minus*)

★ pot marigold seeds (*Calendula officinalis*)

★ cornflower (Bachelor's Button) seeds (*Centaurea cyanus*)

★ a planter at least 15 inches wide, filled with multi-purpose compost

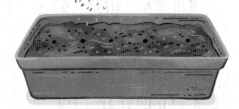

1 Water the compost well. Lay 5 nasturtium seeds on top, spaced out well. Press each one down ¾ of an inch. Scatter on the other seeds. Cover with a little compost.

Harvesting

Pull off a flower and pick off the petals to eat. Throw the rest away.

2 Check every 2-3 days and water if dry. In 2-3 weeks, seedlings will appear. Keep watering. Flowers will grow.

Pick flowers regularly. It helps the plants make more.

Other edible flowers:

You can eat flowers from other plants in this book: squash (pages 38–39), zucchini (pages 42–43) and chives, rosemary and dill (pages 50–51). Don't try eating any other types of flowers, as they might be poisonous.

Bees visit flowers to drink nectar (a sweet liquid) inside them. Tiny grains called 'pollen' brush off on the bees.

The bees spread the pollen from flower to flower, which will make seeds for next year. This is called *pollination*.

Pollen

Nasturtium petals taste slightly spicy.

Water every 2–3 days.

Cut off dead flowers. This helps the plants make more flowers, too.

BABY SALAD LEAVES

It takes time for a whole lettuce head to grow, but it's much quicker if you harvest baby lettuce leaves. You can even sow different types of lettuce, for a variety of baby leaves. Grow lettuce inside or outside.

Sow:
Spring to end of summer

Harvest:
Spring to fall

Site:
Inside, sunny or outside, bright but shaded for part of the day

You will need:

★ lettuce seeds or mixed salad leaf seeds — choose varieties such as Salad Bowl or Red Salad Bowl, or ones labeled 'cut and come again' or 'salad leaf mix'

★ a round planter at least 8 inches wide and 4 inches deep, or a long planter such as a windowbox at least 4 inches wide and deep, filled with multi-purpose compost, plus a drip tray if growing inside

1 Sow around 20 seeds (see page 55), or more if the planter is over 4 inches wide.

2 Check every 2-3 days and water if dry. After 7-10 days, seedlings will appear. Keep watering every 2-3 days.

Potential problems

If the plants get too much hot sun, they may grow flowers. This is called 'bolting' (see page 48). To prevent this, keep the planter in shade for part of the day and don't forget to water it.

Pick off any slugs or snails you see. See page 58 for tips on keeping them away.

Keep watering every 2-3 days, or more often if the weather's hot.

New leaves grow from the middle of each plant.

Remove any plants that are smaller or weaker. You can eat them, too.

Harvesting regularly encourages more leaves to grow.

Harvesting

When the leaves are around 2-4 inches long, cut a few from the outside of each plant.

HANGING STRAWBERRIES

Strawberries grow hanging down, so they are perfect for a hanging basket. It also keeps the strawberries away from hungry slugs and snails. Before you start this project, make sure you have a sunny place to hang the basket.

Plant:
Spring

Harvest:
Summer

Site:
Outside, sunny

You will need:

★ 3 or 4 strawberry plants — choose varieties such as Tristar, Tribute, Mara Des Bois, Evie, or Albion

★ a hanging basket with a liner (or see 'Other containers' opposite)

★ a big plant pot or a bucket

★ a 6 inch square of plastic cut from an old plastic bag, with some holes poked in it using a pencil

★ multi-purpose compost

★ a small plastic plant pot

★ liquid tomato food

1

Balance the hanging basket on the big pot or bucket. Put in the liner. Lay the plastic square in the middle. Fill with compost.

Make sure the central part of each plant is not covered.

2

Plant the strawberry plants (see page 56) around the edge. Push the small plant pot into the compost in the middle. Hang in a sunny place outside.

3

Water really well, pouring the water into the small pot in the middle. After that, water the hanging basket every day, or twice a day if it's warm.

Potential pests

Pick off any slugs or snails you see. Birds also eat strawberries, so pick ripe strawberries right away.

Other containers

You could use a plant pot at least 20 inches tall. Fill with multi-purpose compost and follow steps 2-3 opposite.

Alternatively, use a planter such as a windowbox at least 8 inches wide and tall, on a windowsill or a low wall. Fill with compost and follow steps 2-3.

The plants will hang over the sides. Flowers will appear, then fade.

Strawberries grow where the flowers were. They're green at first.

Keep on watering every day.

After flowers appear, add liquid tomato food to the water once a week, following the instructions on the packaging.

Harvesting

The strawberries are ready when they're bright red. Pull them off gently.

MUSTARD AND CRESS

Mustard and cress are ready to eat in just a week. Grow them inside on a light, bright windowsill in a 'mini greenhouse' made from a jar. They have a peppery taste that's good in salads or sandwiches.

Do:
Anytime

Harvest:
Around 7–8 days after starting

Site:
Inside, light and airy

You will need:

★ cress seeds – choose a variety such as Curled, Extra Curled or Curly Top

★ mustard seeds, for sprouting

★ a clean glass jar with a lid

★ paper towel

1 Fold a piece of paper towel in half. Wet it so it's just damp. Press it into the jar lid – cut to fit if you need to.

2 Sprinkle mustard and cress seeds all over the paper towel. Put in a light place inside.

3 Put the jar over the lid. Check every day to make sure the paper towel is still damp. Wet it if you need to.

4 After a few days, seedlings will grow. When they are ¾ of an inch high, take off the jar. Keep wetting the paper towel to make sure it stays damp.

Home-grown cress tastes spicier than 'salad cress' that you buy.

Mustard is peppery. If you don't like spicy flavors, grow cress on its own.

Harvesting

The mustard and cress are ready when they're around 2 inches high. Cut at the bottom of the stems. Eat right away.

You can grow other types of seeds, such as radish, purple basil or beets, in the same way. Look for packets labeled 'micro-greens'.

Beet   Radish   Purple basil

CLIMBING CUCUMBERS

Cucumbers grow on big, sprawling plants called vines. You can train the vines up canes, so the cucumbers hang down as they grow. Choose a variety that can grow outdoors.

Plant:
Late spring

Harvest:
Late summer

Site:
Outside, sunny and sheltered from wind

1 Wrap the rubber band around the canes. Spread out the ends and push them down into the planter.

Add cane toppers.

The band goes near the top.

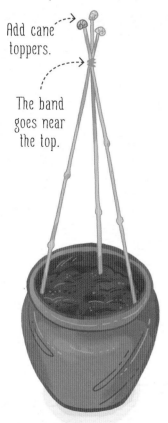

2

Plant the cucumber plant in the middle (see how on page 56). Water well.

3

Check every other day and water if dry. As they grow, gently wind the stems around the canes. Tie them on with string.

You will need:

★ a cucumber plant — choose a compact variety like Spacemaster, Salad Bush Hybrid, Burpless Bush Hybrid, or 'pickling' varieties like Pickle Bush

★ a large planter at least 16 inches tall and 12 inches wide filled with multi-purpose compost

★ 3 canes, at least 6 feet tall

★ rubber band

★ thin string

★ liquid tomato food

Potential pests

Protect from aphids, slugs and snails (see pages 58–59).

If white, powdery patches appear on the leaves, this may be a fungus called powdery mildew. To help avoid it, water regularly.

When the main stems reach the top, cut them off just above a leaf. This will make more cucumbers grow.

Side shoots grow from the main stem. Cut them off just beyond the seventh leaf.

Flowers grow, then wilt. Cucumbers grow in their place.

After flowers appear, add liquid tomato food every 10-14 days when watering (follow the instructions on the packaging).

Water every other day, or every day if it's hot.

Harvesting

The cucumbers are ready when they're around 10 inches long, or 3 inches for pickling varieties. Cut them off carefully.

GROWING FROM PITS

You don't have to buy seeds to grow. You could take seeds from fruit that you eat, such as avocados, dates and citrus fruits, and grow them into plants. It can take years, and a conservatory or hot climate, for these plants to grow any fruit of their own, but in the meantime they make great houseplants.

Plant:
Anytime

Site:
Bright & warm, inside

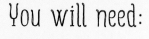

You will need:

★ fresh pit or seeds from ripe, preferably organic fruit (organic seeds are more likely to grow, but you could try non-organic too)

★

★ a plant pot around 3½ inches wide, filled with multi-purpose compost, and a drip tray

★

★ a resealable plastic bag that the pot and drip tray will fit inside

1
Water the compost well. Prepare and plant the pit or seeds (see opposite). Seal the pot and tray in the plastic bag.

2
Check the compost every few days and water if it's dry. In a few weeks, roots, shoots and leaves will grow. Remove the bag.

3

If several seedlings grow, cut away the smaller, weaker ones to leave one strong one.

4
Keep watering regularly as the plant grows. When roots show at the bottom, repot the plant (see page 56). Continue repotting as needed.

Avocado

Preparing

Wash the avocado pit really well. Put in a container and cover with water. Leave for 2 days.

Planting

With the pointed end up, push the pit into the compost.

Leave the top half of the pit uncovered.

Citrus fruit

Preparing

Remove 5 seeds from a lemon, orange or grapefruit.
Put in a sieve. Rub under running water to remove all fruit.

Planting

Use a pencil to make 5 holes in the compost. Push a seed into each so it is ¼ of an inch deep. Cover with a little compost.

Date

Preparing

Use pits from fresh, not dried, dates — fresh dates are juicier and may be labeled 'Medjool'. Wash the pits, put in a container and cover with water. Leave for 2 days.

Planting

Push 2 pits into the compost so they are spaced out well and are 1 inch down. Cover with a little compost.

TOMATO TOWER

Some types of cherry tomatoes grow hanging down. They're known as 'tumbling' tomatoes. Here you can find out how to grow them outdoors in a tower made from two pots.

Plant:
Late spring

Harvest:
Summer

Site:
Outside sunny

You will need:

★ 4 cherry tomato plants — choose a 'tumbling' variety such as Early Bush, Sun Gold, Tumbling Tom, or Patio Princess

★ a plant pot at least 15 inches wide and 12 inches tall

★ a plant pot around 10 inches wide and 8 inches tall

★ multi-purpose compost

★ liquid tomato food

1 Fill the big pot ¾ full of compost. Put the smaller pot on top. Add compost around it, then fill it with compost, too.

2 Plant one tomato plant in the top pot and three in the big pot, spacing them out evenly (see page 56). Water well.

3

Check the compost every day and water if it's dry.

Potential pests

Tomatoes grown outside in this way shouldn't have too many problems with pests.

As the plants grow, they will hang down. Flowers will appear.

Tomatoes grow from the flowers. They're green at first.

Water every day. After flowers appear, add liquid tomato food to the water once a week, according to the instructions on the packaging.

Most tumbling tomatoes turn red when they're ripe.

Some varieties ripen to orange, yellow or striped.

Harvesting

Pull a tomato gently. If it's ripe it will come off easily.

FLYING SAUCER SQUASH

Squash are related to zucchinis and pumpkins. Here you can find out how to grow a type that's known as 'patty pan' or 'flying saucer' squash, because of the shape. It grows well from seed in a pot placed outdoors.

Sow:
Late spring

Harvest:
Late summer

Site:
Outside, sunny

You will need:

★ patty pan squash seeds — choose a variety from your local gardening center

★ a plant pot 17 inches wide filled with multi-purpose compost

★ a small plastic plant pot

★ liquid tomato food

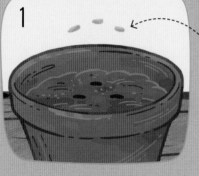

Plant the seeds on their sides.

Plant 3 seeds in the middle, 2 inches apart and ¾ of an inch deep. Water well. Check every other day and water if dry.

In 1-2 weeks, seedlings will appear. When they're 2 inches tall, pull out the smaller ones, leaving one strong one.

Water seeps from the pot into the compost.

3

Push the small pot into the compost at the side. This is for watering the plant. It also stops water from splashing onto the leaves (see 'Potential problems' box).

Potential problems

Protect from slugs and snails (for tips see page 58).

When watering, try not to get any water on the leaves as this might spread powdery mildew fungus — white, powdery patches on the leaves.

Water into the small pot every other day.

After 6-8 weeks, flowers will appear, then wilt.

After flowers appear, mix liquid tomato food into the water every 10-14 days (follow the instructions on the packaging).

After the flowers wilt, squash will start growing.

Harvesting

The squash are ready when they're firm and 2-4 inches across. Cut the stem just above the squash.

Flying saucer squash come in different colors – the seed packet will tell you what to expect.

NEW POTATOES

If you plant a potato, it sprouts into a plant with leaves above the soil and lots more potatoes under the ground. It's best to buy a potato for planting (a 'seed potato'). Potatoes sold for eating might not grow.

Start:
Late winter to early spring

Plant:
Early spring

Harvest:
Summer

Site:
Cool & light inside, then sunny outside

You will need:

★ a 'seed potato' for planting — choose a 'first early' or 'second early' variety such as Charlotte, Lady Cristl, Rocket or Anya

★ a 2 inch section cut from a cardboard tube

★ a pencil

★ a 2½-gallon bag of multi-purpose compost

★ multi-purpose liquid plant food (not tomato food)

1 Stand the potato in the cardboard tube on a windowsill inside, not in direct sun. Wait until a 1 inch long shoot grows.

2 Outdoors, use the pencil to poke 20 holes in the bottom of the compost bag. Cut open the top. Empty out the top 8 inches of compost. Put the potato in the middle.

Keep the shoots at the top.

Leave a 2 inch gap at the top of the bag.

3 Put back most of the compost. Water well. Check once a week (more often in hot weather) and water if the compost is dry.

Potential problems

If potatoes show at the surface of the compost, cover them with extra compost. This is called 'earthing up' and will prevent them from turning green and poisonous.

Tall stems and leaves grow. Sometimes flowers appear.

Apart from potatoes, all parts of potato plants are poisonous, so don't ever eat them.

Water every few days (every day if it's hot).

Once every two weeks, add liquid plant food to the water (follow the instructions on the packaging).

Roots grow down. The ends swell into new potatoes.

Harvesting

When the leaves wilt and the stems droop, tip over the bag. Feel around in the compost for the potatoes.

ZUCCHINI

Zucchini need plenty of water and food to make them grow well. Here you can find out how to grow them in a grow bag (a compost-filled bag to grow plants in). Look for interesting yellow or striped zucchini when buying your seeds.

Sow:
Late spring

Harvest:
Summer to early fall

Site:
Outside, sunny

You will need:

★ zucchini seeds — choose a variety such as Ambassador, Greyzini, Bushbaby or Aristocrat

★ a grow bag

★ a sharp pencil

★ scissors

★ 2 plant pots around 4 inches wide

★ liquid tomato food

1 Poke 10 big drainage holes in the bottom of the grow bag. Turn it over and put it outside in the sun.

2 Using scissors, slit along the middle of the grow bag. At each end plant 2 seeds, 2 inches apart and ¾ of an inch deep. Water well.

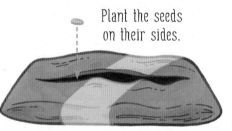

Plant the seeds on their sides.

Good and bad bugs

★ Protect from slugs and snails (see page 58).

★ Encourage bees by planting marigolds nearby (see pages 24-25).

3 Check every other day. Water if dry. In 2-3 weeks, seedlings will appear. Wait until they're 2 inches high. Pull out the weaker one at each end.

Water soaks into the compost from the pots.

4 Press in the plant pots 2 inches away from each remaining seedling. Check the compost every day. If dry, pour water into the pots (this helps to prevent powdery mildew — see page 38).

Leaves will spread beyond the grow bag.

After 6-8 weeks, flowers will appear.

After the flowers wilt, zucchini start growing.

Every 10-14 days, mix liquid tomato food with water (follow the instructions on the packaging) and pour into the pots.

Harvesting

Harvest zucchini when firm and 4-5 inches long. Cut them off the vine.

RASPBERRIES

Fall-fruiting raspberries are the easiest type to grow. The plants are often known as 'canes'. You plant them outdoors when it's cold, then cut them down. Next spring and summer, shoots, leaves and raspberries grow.

Plant:
Early fall or late winter

Harvest:
Late summer to early fall

Site:
Sunny, outside

You will need:

★ 3 raspberry canes — choose fall-fruiting varieties such as Autumn bliss, Caroline, or Heritage (they may come with bare roots or in pots)

★ a large planter at least 16 inches tall and wide, filled with multi-purpose compost

★ 3 bamboo canes, around 5 feet high

★ string

★ bird netting

★ liquid tomato food

1 For bare-root raspberry canes, soak them in a bucket of water for 2 hours. Take the top 4 inches of compost out of the planter. Plant the canes in the pot, spacing them out well, then cover with 2 inches of compost. Water well.

Spread out the roots before you cover them.

2 If you buy raspberry canes in pots rather than bare-root canes, plant them (see how on page 56), spacing them around the planter. Water well.

3 Cut each cane so just ½ an inch shows. Water twice a week if dry. Wait until shoots grow in spring.

4 Once the shoots are 3 feet high, push the bamboo canes around the edge of the pot. Wrap and tie string around the tops and middles. Keep watering twice a week if dry.

Add cane toppers.

Flowers grow, then fade. Raspberries grow in their place.

After flowers appear, water every other day (every day if it's hot). Every 10-14 days add liquid tomato food to the water (follow the instructions on the packaging).

Harvesting

When a raspberry is ripe, you can pull it off its stalk easily.

In the winter, cut the raspberry canes down to ½ an inch. They will grow again in spring.

When the flowers fade, spread bird netting over everything to keep birds off (see page 59).

POPCORN

Popcorn is made from the seeds (or 'kernels') of corn plants. Some varieties of corn are grown especially for popping, and come in interesting colors. Grow them outdoors in pots — they will grow very tall!

You will need:

★ sweet corn seeds — choose a variety such as Black, Gold Hybrid, Peppy, or White Cloud

★ 4 small pots around 2½ inches wide, filled with multi-purpose compost, with drip trays

★ a planter at least 19 inches wide and 12 inches deep, filled with multi-purpose compost

★ frost fabric

★ string

Sow:
Spring

Plant:
Early summer

Harvest:
Late summer to early fall

Site:
Inside sunny, then outside sunny

1
Push two seeds into each small pot. Water well. Put inside on a sunny windowsill. Check every other day. Water if dry. In around 2 weeks, seedlings will grow.

Don't throw the seed packet away! You'll need it when you make popcorn (see opposite).

Tassels grow at the top. They are flowers and make pollen.

Pollen blows down onto threads called silks. This makes corn cobs grow.

When the tassels are tall and yellow, help the pollen drop by shaking the plant gently.

The cobs are ready when the silks turn brown.

2

When they're 2 inches tall, pull out the weaker plant from each pot. Cover with frost fabric tied on with string. Put outside in the sun. After a week, remove the fabric.

In hot weather, water every day.

3 In early summer, plant the seedlings (page 56) in the planter, 8½ inches apart. Check every other day. Water if dry.

Protect from slugs and snails – see page 58.

Harvesting

Cut a cob off a plant, close to the stem. Peel off the papery outer leaves.

Popcorn

The seed packet will have instructions on how to dry the cobs and cook the popcorn.

RAINBOW CHARD

Chard (also known as Swiss chard) is green and leafy with brightly colored stems. Some packets of seeds grow a mixture of stem colors — this is known as 'rainbow' chard. Grow it in a planter outdoors.

Sow:
Spring and summer

Harvest:
Summer to winter

Site:
Outside, sunny but shady in the afternoon

You will need:

★ rainbow chard seeds — choose a variety such as Bright Lights or Ruby Red

★ a planter at least 12 inches wide, filled with multi-purpose compost

1 Water well. Place 6 seeds so they're 2 inches apart. Cover with a layer of compost ½ an inch thick.

2 Check the compost every other day and water if dry. After 2-3 weeks, seedlings will appear. Keep watering every other day.

3 When the seedlings are 1½ inches high, cut away the weaker ones to leave around three at least 4 inches apart. Keep watering every other day — don't let the compost dry out.

Bolting

When plants grow flowers, rather than leaves, it's known as bolting. It happens if they get too hot or dry. If you see a long stem with a flower bud, cut it off near the plant's base. Water regularly to avoid bolting, but it may happen anyway at the end of the plant's life.

Potential pests

Slugs, snails, aphids and caterpillars like chard. See pages 58-59 for how to deter them.

You can eat both the leaves and stems of chard plants.

Pick a few stems at a time from the *outside* of each plant. This will help the plants to keep growing.

All the stems on one plant are the same color.

Make sure the plants are in shade for part of the day and water well, to help prevent them from bolting (see opposite page).

Harvesting

When the leaves are 2 inches long or more, they're ready.

HERB GARDEN

You can grow herbs, such as thyme, rosemary, chives and dill, all together in a sunny spot outdoors, or inside, on a sunny windowsill.

Plant:
Spring

Harvest:
Summer to fall

Site:
Sunny inside or outside

You will need:

★ a thyme plant or an edible sage plant (*Salvia officinalis*)

★ a rosemary plant (you could use a plant grown from a cutting — see pages 22-23)

★ chive seeds

★ dill seeds

★ a large planter such as a windowbox or pot at least 16 inches wide and 10 inches deep, filled with multi-purpose compost

1 Plant the thyme or sage and the rosemary on opposite sides of the planter (see page 56). Water well.

2 Sprinkle 12 chive seeds in one patch. Sprinkle 12 dill seeds in another patch. Cover with a thin layer of compost.

3 Water well. Check the compost every few days and water if it's dry. In 2-3 weeks, seedlings should appear.

Helpful herbs

Some garden pests dislike the strong smell of herbs. If pests attack a plant, move it next to your herb planter. The pests might go away.

The dill will grow feathery leaves.

Some herbs flower in spring, others in summer. Bees love to visit the flowers.

The chives will grow into tall, grass-like stems.

Harvesting

Only harvest a small amount at a time from each plant.

Sage: pull off individual leaves.

Chives: cut a bunch of stems off at the bottom.

Thyme, rosemary or dill: cut off the top 2-4 inches of a few stems.

Keep on watering every few days, if dry.

TIPS AND TECHNIQUES

In this section, you'll find essential techniques needed for many of the projects, such as how to fill a container and sow seeds. There are also lots of useful tips — when to water plants, how to deal with garden pests, and even how to make your own compost and plant food.

FILLING CONTAINERS

For many of the projects in this book, you'll need to fill a plant pot or other container with compost. Find out how to do this here.

Always use the type of compost and size of container described in the list.

Filling a small pot

1 Use the pot to scoop up some compost.

2 Put the pot over a plastic bag to catch any falling compost, so you can reuse it.

3 Break up any lumps in the compost. Level the surface gently.

Filling a large planter

Use a small pot or a trowel to scoop the compost.

1 Put the planter in the place where you want your plants to grow (it will be heavy when it's full).

2 Scoop compost into the planter. Leave a 1 inch gap at the top.

3 Break up any lumps in the compost. Level the surface gently.

SOWING SEEDS

For some of the projects, you start by sowing (planting) seeds. Find out here how to handle different types of seeds.

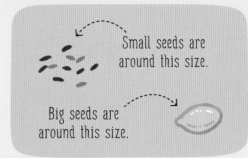

Small seeds are around this size.

Big seeds are around this size.

Small seeds

The seeds will drop out gradually.

1 Pinch around 5 seeds between your thumb and first finger. Move your hand slowly in a zig-zag, rubbing your finger and thumb.

2 Do this again and again, until you have sown the number of seeds listed in the project.

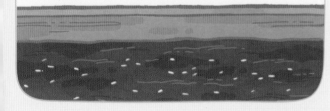

3 Sprinkle on a ½ inch layer of compost. Water well.

Use a 'rose' attachment on the watering can to make the water gentler.

Big seeds

1 Water the compost well.

2 Take one seed and push it into the compost, as far down as the growing instructions tell you to.

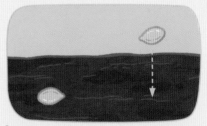

3 Push the compost over the hole to cover it, then gently press it down. Make sure you leave at least 4 inches between seeds.

PLANTING AND REPOTTING

When you buy a plant in a pot, you need to plant it in a bigger container right away. You also need to do this with plants that have become too big for their pots — this is called 'repotting'.

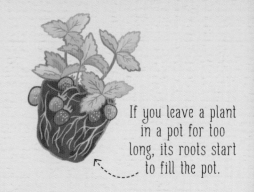

If you leave a plant in a pot for too long, its roots start to fill the pot.

Planting

Keep the scooped-out compost.

1 Use a small pot or trowel to scoop a hole the same size as the plant you're planting.

Fingers on either side of the stem

2 Hold the plant like this. Gently pull away the pot (squeeze or wiggle the pot if it's stuck).

3 Put the plant in the hole. Use the scooped-out compost to fill gaps at the sides and top. Gently press down.

Repotting

1 If roots start to show at the bottom of a pot, the plant needs to be repotted.

2 Choose a pot at least one size bigger than the one the plant is in. Fill it with multi-purpose compost (see page 54).

3 Follow steps 1–3 above to move the plant to the new pot. When roots show again, repot again.

WATERING

All plants need water to survive. Here you can find out the best way to water your plants, to help keep them healthy.

Some plants like more water, some less. Each growing project tells you how often to water.

When?

★ Every other day (or every day if it's hot and sunny) poke a finger into the compost. If it feels dry, water it (see below).

★ If a plant's leaves or stems are drooping, water its compost immediately.

★ Water plants in the cooler morning or evening. When the sun is hotter, it can dry up the water before the plant gets enough.

How?

★ Always water onto the compost, not the leaves or flowers. Water on leaves can make them shrivel and die, or turn moldy.

★ For outside plants, water until water comes out of the bottom of the pot. For inside plants, water until the drip tray fills. After one hour, empty the tray.

You could make your own plant food – see page 61.

★ Some projects ask you to add liquid plant food when watering. For store-bought food, follow the instructions on the packaging carefully.

PESKY PESTS

Some animals eat or damage plants. Here are some tips to help keep the most common ones away from your plants.

Snails and slugs

These slimy beasts munch on juicy leaves, such as lettuce.

Pick off any slugs or snails that are on or near your plants.

Grow chives next to juicy-leaved plants. Slugs and snails dislike the strong smell.

Surround plants with a prickly layer of broken eggshells, grit or sand. Slugs and snails won't like to cross it.

Caterpillars

Caterpillars are the young of butterflies and moths. They eat holes in leaves and flowers of plants such as nasturtiums and salad leaves.

Older plants are usually able to cope with a caterpillar attack. Put on gloves and pick any caterpillars off younger plants.

Leave some caterpillars to grow into butterflies. They can help to pollinate plants.

Birds

Birds are helpful as they eat pests such as caterpillars, snails and slugs. But they may also eat crops such as berries and peas.

Aphids and whiteflies

Aphids are tiny insects that suck juices, called sap, from the leaves and stems of plants such as beans and nasturtiums. Whiteflies are small white insects with wings. They feed on sap too.

Cover any vulnerable plants with bird netting – plastic mesh with small holes.

Tie bird netting to canes so that it stands away from the plant. This will stop birds from taking fruit through the netting.

Adult hoverfly

Grow dill near vulnerable plants. Dill attracts ladybugs and young hoverflies, which eat aphids.

Ladybug

Hoverfly young

If you want to lure aphids away from beans, you could plant a nasturtium nearby.

Black aphid

Green aphid

Cats

Cats won't eat your plants, but in larger planters they may uproot plants and leave messes.

Poke small canes into the compost to keep cats off. Add cane toppers.

Fill a clean spray bottle with water. Spray aphids and whiteflies, to blast them off the plant.

Whiteflies

Gently wipe off any aphids or whiteflies with a paper towel too.

Put orange or lemon peel in the planter. The smell may deter cats.

COMPOST AND PLANT FOOD

You could buy compost and plant food for most projects in this book, or make your own. These pages show you how. Always use store-bought compost for sowing seeds.

Compost

You can make compost from a mixture of old plants ('greens') and paper and cardboard ('browns'). Don't add cooked food, meat, fish, cheese, bones, parts of diseased plants, hard stems or wood.

Compost needs shade in summer.

Greens

Fruit and vegetable peelings

Grass cutings

Soft, small trimmings from garden plants

Browns

Dry fall leaves

Straw

Small pieces of newspaper and cardboard

You could use a compost bin with an open base.

For a compost heap or bin, make a thick layer of browns, then a thin layer of greens, and so on. Wet each layer as you make it.

Cover with thick cardboard.

Once a month, mix and turn everything. If it's dry, add water. Scrape back into a heap and cover again.

It's ready after 6 months to a year, when it's dark, crumbly and smells like fresh soil.

Plant food

Weeds soaked in water make an effective plant food (but not for projects that ask for liquid tomato food). You need a plastic plant pot with drainage holes and a bucket with a tightly fitting lid.

Collect weed leaves. Put in the plastic plant pot.

Put the pot in the bucket. Add water to cover. Put on the lid.

Wait 6 weeks. Lift up the plant pot so the liquid drains into the bucket.

Warning! Hold your nose! Very smelly!

Put one cup of the liquid in a watering can. Add 10 cups of water.

Use it to water your plants.

Leaf mold

This is a simple compost made from dead fall leaves. It's simpler to make than ordinary compost, but may take longer.

Collect dead fall leaves. Wait until it rains, or wet them with a watering can.

Put them in a plastic lawn bag. Poke holes in the bag.

Put in a sheltered spot. Wait for one or two years.

It's ready when it's dark, crumbly and smells like fresh soil.

Add a little to bought compost to the leaf mold when planting or repotting, to keep it moist and healthy.

GLOSSARY

This glossary explains some useful gardening words that are used in the book.

aphids Small bugs that swarm onto plants and feed on sap (see *sap*). Aphids can stop a plant from growing properly.

baby leaves Leaves that are picked before they're fully grown.

bare-root When a plant is sold without its roots in compost.

bird netting A mesh that's placed over fruit plants to stop birds from eating it.

bolting When some leafy vegetable plants start to die and grow long stems, flowers and seeds.

bud A young flower, before it's opened.

carrot flies Small flies whose young eat into carrots.

compost Broken down plant material, cardboard or paper that makes a substance for plants to grow in.

cut and come again A type of lettuce or other leafy vegetable that can grow more leaves when some of its leaves are cut.

cutting A stem or part of a stem that's cut from a plant and used to grow a new plant.

downy mildew A disease that is a yellow or pale green fungus growing on the leaves or stems of plants.

drip tray A dish placed under a plant pot to collect any water that seeps through the compost.

earthing up Covering growing potatoes with compost to stop them from getting too much sunlight.

edible flowers Flowers that you can eat.

frost fabric A thin fabric draped over plants to keep them warm or protect them from pests.

fruit canes Fruit-producing plants that need netting or bamboo canes for support, because they don't have strong stems.

garden pest A bug or animal that eats or attacks plants, weakening them, or killing them completely.

gardener-friendly bug A bug that helps plants to grow by spreading pollen or by eating pests that attack plants.

grow bag A compost-filled bag in which plants can be grown.

hanging basket A hanging container used to grow plants with trailing stems.

harvesting Picking leaves, seeds, vegetables or fruits when they're ready to eat or use.

herb A plant with a strong, tangy smell and taste. Herbs are often used in cooking.

micro-greens A plant that's picked after its first leaves grow.

mold A disease caused by a plant getting too wet, or its roots sitting in water.

nectar A sweet liquid inside a plant. Bees and butterflies feed on it.

new potatoes Types of potatoes that are ready to harvest when they're still small.

patty pan A type of small squash that is round with curvy egdes, similar to a flying saucer.

pea netting A mesh that's used for peas to grow up.

pit A seed inside a fruit.

plant food Something that's given to plants to help them grow.

pollen A powder inside flowers. When pollen is spread from one flower to another, it makes the plant grow new seeds, fruits or vegetables.

pollination When pollen is spread from flower to flower, either by the bugs or the wind.

powdery mildew A disease that is a white fungus growing on the leaves and stems of a plant.

repotting Moving a plant from a smaller pot into a bigger one.

ripe When a fruit, vegetable or seed on a plant is fully grown and ready to be picked.

root Part of a plant that grows down into the compost and sucks up water and food. Some roots such as carrots grow into vegetables.

rust A disease that is a red or orange fungus growing on the leaves of plants, usually shallots, onions and leeks.

sap The liquid inside plants. Aphids and some other pests feed on sap.

seed potato A potato that's planted to grow a new potato plant.

seedling A young plant, usually with only a few leaves and a short stem.

sets Onions, shallots and leeks that are planted to grow new ones.

shoot A new stem, either after it's just grown above the surface of the compost, or from an existing stem.

sowing Planting a seed in compost.

sprouting beans Beans or seeds that are soaked in water until they just start to grow. The whole bean and seed and its shoot are eaten.

tumbling tomato A type of tomato that grows hanging down rather than on upright stems.

vine A long, trailing stem that some vegetable or fruit plants grow.

whiteflies Small white bugs that swarm onto a plant and suck out the sap (see *sap*). Whiteflies can stop plants from growing properly.

INDEX

Additional editorial material by Emily Bone
Design Manager: Nickey Butler   Edited by Jane Chisholm
Digital manipulation by John Russell   American Editor: Carrie Armstrong

First published in 2017 by Usborne Publishing Ltd., Usborne House, 83-85 Saffron Hill, London EC1N 8RT, England.
www.usborne.com Copyright © 2017 Usborne Publishing Ltd. All rights reserved. No part of this publication may be reproduced, stored in a retrieval system or transmitted in any form or by any means, electronic, mechanical, photocopying, recording or otherwise, without the prior permission of the publisher. The name Usborne and the devices ♀ ⊕ are Trade Marks of Usborne Publishing Ltd. AE. First published in America 2017.